FAMILY PRAYERS
FOR ALL OCCASIONS

Harold Shaw Publishers
Wheaton, Illinois

Copyright © 1995 by Harold Shaw Publishers
Compiled by Carol Plueddemann and Vinita Hampton Wright

ISBN 0-87788-645-8
Cover photo © 1995 by Harold Shaw Publishers
Cover and inside design © 1995 by David LaPlaca

Library of Congress Cataloging-in-Publication Data

Prayers around the family table.
    Family prayers for all occasions / compiled by Carol Plueddeman and Vinita Hampton Wright.
        p.   cm.
    Originally published: Prayers around the family. 1991.
    ISBN 0-87788-654-8
    1. Family–Prayer-books and devotions–English. 2. Devotional calendars. I. Plueddeman, Carol. II. Wright, Vinita Hampton, 1958- . III. Title.
    [BV255.P79 1995]
249–dc20   95-7917
                                                                CIP

02   01   00   99   98   97   96   95

10   9   8   7   6   5   4   3   2   1

CONTENTS

Topics

Topics continued on next page

Holidays

Table Graces

ACKNOWLEDGMENTS

We gratefully acknowledge the use of the following resources:

Praise God: Common Prayer at Taizé. New York: Oxford University Press, 1977.

A Diary of Private Prayer by John Baillie. New York: Charles Scribner's Sons, 1949.

Solzhenitsyn: A Pictorial Autobiography. New York: Farrar, Straus, & Giroux, 1974.

The Prayers of Peter Marshall. New York: McGraw-Hill Book Company, Inc., 1954.

Life in the Spirit by Mother Teresa of Calcutta. San Francisco: Harper & Row Publishers, 1983.

Loving Your Preborn Baby by Carol Van Klompenburg & Elizabeth Siitari. Wheaton, Ill: Harold Shaw Publishers, 1990.

Pocket Praise by Robert C. Savage. Wheaton, Ill.: Tyndale House Publishers, Inc., 1985.

Promises of Encouragement. Wheaton, Ill.: Harold Shaw Publishers, 1991.

Flirting with the World by John White. Wheaton, Ill.: Harold Shaw Publishers, 1982.

The Weather of the Heart by Madeleine L'Engle. Wheaton, Ill.: Harold Shaw Publishers, 1978.

TOPICS

in alphabetical order

Remember how the LORD your God led you all the way in the desert these forty years, to humble you and to test you in order to know what was in your heart, whether or not you would keep his commands. He humbled you, causing you to hunger and then feeding you with manna . . . to teach you that man does not live on bread alone but on every word that comes from the mouth of the LORD. Your clothes did not wear out and your feet did not swell during these forty years. Know then in your heart that as a man disciplines his sons, so the LORD your God disciplines you. Observe the commands of the LORD your God, walking in his ways and revering him. For the LORD your God is bringing you into a good land—a land with streams and pools of water, with springs flowing in the valleys and hills.

Deuteronomy 8:2-7

How easy for me to live with you, O Lord! How easy for me to believe in you! When my mind parts in bewilderment or falters, when the most intelligent people see no further than this day's end and do not know what must be done tomorrow, you grant me the serene certitude that you exist and that you will take care that not all the paths of good be closed. Atop the ridge of earthly fame, I look back in wonder at the path which I alone could never have found, a wondrous path through despair to this point from which I, too, could transmit to mankind a reflection of your rays. And as much as I must still reflect you will give me. But as much as I cannot take up you will have already assigned to others.

Aleksandr Solzhenitsyn (b. 1918)

Think back on a part of your life that you see more clearly now than when you were going through it.

s for man, his days are like grass, he flourishes like a flower of the field; the wind blows over it and it is gone, and its place remembers it no more.

But from everlasting to everlasting the LORD'S love is with those who fear him, and his righteousness with their children's children— with those who keep his covenant and remember to obey his precepts.

Psalm 103:15-18

How quickly the seasons pass! No sooner has nature reached the maturity of summer than harvest has come and the cycle of decay and rebirth begins again. The fields are now shorn of their produce; the beauties of the garden are withered; the woods are changing their vegetation, and the trees shedding their foliage—we also never continue in one state. Many of our circumstances and comforts have already dropped away from us, while we ourselves fade like flowers that are here today and gone tomorrow. Blessed be the God and Father of our Lord Jesus Christ for that inheritance that will never fade away. We thank you for the gift of everlasting life.

Albert Barnes (1798-1870), adapted

What do you like most about autumn? Least? How can God's everlasting love be a comfort to you?

his is why since I heard of this faith of yours in the Lord Jesus and the love which you bear towards fellow-Christians, I thank God continually for you and I never give up praying for you; and this is my prayer. That the God of our Lord Jesus Christ, the all-glorious Father, will give you spiritual wisdom and the insight to know more of him: that you may receive that inner illumination of the spirit which will make you realize how great is the hope to which he is calling you—the magnificence and splendour of the inheritance promised to Christians.

Ephesians 1:15-18, PHILLIPS

Dear God, life passes so quickly, and yet we must live it one day, one week, one year at a time. We must grow slowly and work steadily to become all that you want us to be. Thank you for all the special graces that have been present in (name)'s life this year. Thank you for the goals reached and for the growth of character that can be difficult but is so rewarding when it comes. Give (name) the eyes to see your hand in his/her life, and the ability to walk by faith, not by sight. Fill him/her with a spirit of hope, joy, and confidence. We thank you for the memories of the past year and for those that are to come. Help us to appreciate the many ways you touch our lives. Amen.

Think of a special quality you appreciate about the birthday person, and share it with him or her.

My son, do not forget my teaching, but keep my commands in your heart, for they will prolong your life many years and bring you prosperity. Let love and faithfulness never leave you; bind them around your neck, write them on the tablet of your heart. Then you will win favor and a good name in the sight of God and man. Trust in the LORD with all your heart and lean not on your own understanding; in all your ways acknowledge him, and he will make your paths straight.

Proverbs 3:1-6

Lord, this is a special day, because you have given (name) (age) years with us, years filled with discovery and growth and wonderful memories. We ask that you continue to bless (name) with your love and help him/her to live as Jesus lived, loving you and learning to love others. Give him/her success in school, cause his/her body to grow healthy and strong. Most of all, help him/her know that you are with him/her always, and help him/her to trust you more every day and to make wise choices. In Jesus' name, Amen.

What was a favorite time or aspect of your growing-up years?

CONFESSION

If anyone would come after me, he must deny himself and take up his cross daily and follow me. For whoever wants to save his life will lose it, but whoever loses his life for me will save it. What good is it for a man to gain the whole world, and yet lose or forfeit his very self?

Luke 9:23-25

O God, the Light of every heart that sees you, the Life of every soul that loves you, the Strength of every mind that looks for you, help us to continue steadfastly in your holy love. Be the joy of our hearts; take us over and live inside us. The houses of our souls, we confess, are too narrow for you—make them large enough to accommodate your Holy Spirit. They are in ruins—repair them and make them worthy of your presence. They store things that are offensive to you; we know this, but who can help us clean up our lives and put them into order—who but you? It is to you, then, that we cry, asking that you cleanse us from our many secret faults. Keep your servants from presumptuous sins, so that evil cannot control us. Amen.

St. Augustine (354-430), adapted

In today's American culture, what might Jesus have said to convey the same meaning as "Take up your cross"?

Then Moses said, "If your Presence does not go with us, do not send us up from here. How will anyone know that you are pleased with me and with your people unless you go with us? What else will distinguish me and your people from all the other people on the face of the earth?" And the LORD said to Moses, "I will do the very thing you have asked, because I am pleased with you and I know you by name."

Exodus 33:15-17

With all our hearts and souls, O God, we thank you, that in all the changes and chances of this mortal life, we can look up to you and cheerfully submit our wills to yours. We have trusted you, O Father, with ourselves; our souls are in your hand, and we have confidence that you will preserve us from all evil; our bodies, and all that belong to them, are of much less value. We do therefore, trust all that we have to you, with great confidence and satisfaction. We are convinced that tribulation, heartbreak, persecution, famine, poverty, danger, war, the death that we may fear, the life that we may hope for, the present trials that seem to overwhelm—none of these things are reason enough to walk outside of your holy will. Amen.

Thomas Wilson, adapted

Moses knew where God was according to where the pillars of cloud and fire were. What evidence do you see today of God's presence and guidance?

o do not worry, saying, "What shall we eat?" or "What shall we drink?" or "What shall we wear?" For the pagans run after all these things, and your heavenly Father knows that you need them. But seek first his kingdom and his righteousness, and all these things will be given to you as well. Therefore do not worry about tomorrow, for tomorrow will worry about itself. Each day has enough trouble of its own.

Matthew 6:31-33

O Lord, whose way is perfect, help us to always trust in your goodness, that walking with you and following you in all simplicity, we may possess quiet and contented minds; and may cast all our care on you, for you care about us. Please fill us with true worship and gratitude for all that you are for us, to us, and in us. Fill us with love, joy, peace, and all the fruits of the Spirit. Amen.

Christina G. Rossetti (1830-1894), adapted

Under what circumstances have you been most easily swayed from your trust in God?

raise the LORD. Praise him, sun and moon, praise him, all you shining stars.

Praise him, you highest heavens and you waters above the skies.

Let them praise the name of the LORD, for he commanded and they were created.

He set them in place for ever and ever; he gave a decree that will never pass away.

Psalm 148:1a, 3-6

Thanks for Creation

O God, we thank you for this earth, our home; for the wide sky
and the blessed sun, for the salt sea and the running water,
for the everlasting hills and the never-resting winds, for trees
and the common grass underfoot.

We thank you for our senses by which we hear the songs of
birds, and see the splendour of the summer fields, and taste
of the autumn fruits, and rejoice in the feel of the snow, and
smell the breath of the spring.

Grant us a heart wide open to all this beauty; and save our souls
from being so blind that we pass unseeing when even the
common thornbush is aflame with your glory, O God our
creator, who lives and reigns for ever and ever.

Walter Rauschenbusch (1861-1918)

*What aspects of nature do you enjoy the most? Does creation help you feel
closer to God? Why?*

May the Lord show mercy to the household of Onesiphorus, because he often refreshed me and was not ashamed of my chains. On the contrary, when he was in Rome, he searched hard for me until he found me. . . . You know very well in how many ways he helped me in Ephesus.

2 Timothy 1:16-18

Father, we are so grateful to have (name) with us. Thank you for the safe journey here, and we ask for a safe return. May this be a time of sweet fellowship, the sharing of important memories, and the opening of our hearts one to another. We thank you that in your kingdom our love is not limited by time, space, or distance, and that words and experiences that pass between us can last throughout eternity and give us encouragement and joy when we are apart. Bless our meal together. Thank you for this time of celebration. Amen.

Think of an important event or funny incident that has transpired since this person last visited.

They gave Moses this account: "We went into the land to which you sent us, and it does flow with milk and honey! Here is its fruit. But the people who live there are powerful, and the cities are fortified and very large. We even saw descendants of Anak there. . . . We seemed like grasshoppers in our own eyes, and we looked the same to them."

Joshua son of Nun and Caleb son of Jephunneh, who were among those who had explored the land . . . said to the entire Israelite assembly, "The land we passed through and explored is exceedingly good. If the LORD is pleased with us, he will lead us into that land, a land flowing with milk and honey, and will give it to us. Only do not rebel against the LORD. And do not be afraid of the people of the land, because we will swallow them up. Their protection is gone, but the LORD is with us. Do not be afraid of them."

Numbers 13:27–14:9

O God, our heavenly Father, we your children come now to you with our requests. We cannot live without your blessing. Life is too hard for us and our task is too large. We get discouraged, and our hands and heads hang limp and despondent. We come to you with our weakness, asking you for strength. Help us to rejoice always. Let us not be disheartened by difficulties. Let us never doubt your love or any of your promises. Give us grace to be encouragers of others, never discouragers. Let us not go about with sadness or fear among people, but may we be your blessing to everyone we meet, always making life easier, never harder, for those who come within our influence. Help us to be as Christ to others, that they may see something of His love in our lives and learn to love Him in us. Please hear us and receive our prayer, and forgive our sins, for Jesus Christ's sake. Amen.

A.R. Miffer, adapted

What makes encouragement such a powerful force in our lives?

D o not love the world or anything in the world. If anyone loves the world, the love of the Father is not in him. For everything in the world—the cravings of sinful man, the lust of his eyes, and the boasting of what he has and does—comes not from the Father but from the world. The world and its desires pass away, but the man who does the will of God lives forever.

1 John 2:15-17

Almighty God, who has placed us in this world and from whom we daily receive so many blessings, help us to pass our time with a view to eternity and eager to accomplish your will. We pray that the benefits and blessings that first drew us to you will not become snares to hold us to this world, but may stimulate us to reverence your name and appreciate your mercy. Help us to know you confidently as our God and strive on our part to be your people, and so to dedicate ourselves and all our services to you, that your name may be honored by our attitudes and behavior. Amen.

John Calvin (1509-1564), adapted

How do you know when you are "loving the world" too much?

Be strong and courageous, because you will lead these people to inherit the land I swore to their forefathers to give them. Be strong and very courageous. Be careful to obey all the law my servant Moses gave you: do not turn from it to the right or to the left, that you may be successful wherever you go. Do not let this Book of the Law depart from your mouth; meditate on it day and night, so that you may be careful to do everything written in it. Then you will be prosperous and successful. Have I not commanded you? Be strong and courageous. Do not be terrified; do not be discouraged, for the LORD your God will be with you wherever you go.

Joshua 1:6-9

Give us, O Lord, steadfast hearts that cannot be dragged down by false loves; give us courageous hearts that cannot be worn down by trouble; give us righteous hearts that cannot be sidetracked by unholy or unworthy goals. Give to us also, our Lord and God, understanding to know you, diligence to look for you, wisdom to recognize you, and a faithfulness that will bring us to see you face to face. Amen.

St. Thomas Aquinas (1225?-1274), adapted

How does society generally view a person who is truly faithful to a specific cause?

o not store up for yourselves treasures on earth, where moth and rust destroy, and where thieves break in and steal. But store up for yourselves treasures in heaven, where moth and rust do not destroy, and where thieves do not break in and steal. For where your treasure is, there your heart will be also.

Matthew 6:19-21

Heavenly Father, how wonderful is the capacity to grow and to learn, to discover truth in the world, and add good knowledge to our lives. Today we especially thank you for this important milestone in (name)'s life. We thank you for the rewards of hard work and persistent study. We thank you for all the possibilities that lie ahead and that by your grace we can have a future and a hope. In the years to come, Lord, remind (name) of all the gifts he/she has so freely received from you. Give him/her the courage and strength to persevere through tasks and to achieve goals. But most of all, we pray for the molding and perfecting of character that comes only from the work of the Holy Spirit as we allow him free reign in our hearts. Take this life, Lord, and guide it, ever protecting (name) in your loving arms.

What words of wisdom would you pass on to someone who is graduating?

e believe that Jesus died and rose again and so we believe that God will bring with Jesus those who have fallen asleep in him. According to the Lord's own word, we tell you that we who are still alive, who are left till the coming of the Lord, will certainly not precede those who have fallen asleep. For the Lord himself will come down from heaven, with a loud command, with the voice of the archangel and with the trumpet call of God, and the dead in Christ will rise first. After that, we who are still alive and are left will be caught up together with them in the clouds to meet the Lord in the air. And so we will be with the Lord forever. Therefore encourage each other with these words.

1 Thessalonians 4:14-18

Grant us courage Lord, at the death of this person we loved, to meet each day with steadfast faith in your goodness. Help us not to sorrow without hope, but in thankful remembrance of a life that touched ours and in expectation of that great reunion when all the dead shall rise, and we will all live forever in your presence.

From *Promises of Encouragement*

How do you deal with death and dying? What brings you comfort in these times?

nswer me quickly, O LORD; my spirit fails.

Do not hide your face from me or I will be like those who go down to the pit.

Let the morning bring me word of your unfailing love; for I have put my trust in you.

Show me the way I should go, for to you I lift up my soul.

Rescue me from my enemies, O LORD, for I hide myself in you.

Teach me to do your will, for you are my God; may your good Spirit lead me on level ground.

Psalm 143:7-10

O God, who guides the meek in judgment, and by whom light rises up in darkness for the godly; grant us, in all our doubts and uncertainties the grace to ask what you would have us to do; that the Spirit of wisdom may save us from all false choices, and that in your light we may see light, and in your straight path we may not stumble, through Jesus Christ our Lord. Amen.

William Bright (1824-1901), adapted

In what ways does God help you make wise choices?

I will remain in the world no longer, but they are still in the world, and I am coming to you. Holy Father, protect them by the power of your name—the name you gave me—so that they may be one as we are one. . . . I am coming to you now, but I say these things while I am still in the world, so that they may have the full measure of my joy within them. I have given them your word and the world has hated them, for they are not of the world any more than I am of the world. My prayer is not that you take them out of the world but that you protect them from the evil one. They are not of the world, even as I am not of it. Sanctify them by the truth; your word is truth. As you sent me into the world, I have sent them into the world. For them I sanctify myself, that they too may be truly sanctified.

John 17:11, 13-19

Our Father, grant us, this day, the sense of your presence to lift us up, your light to direct us, and strength for your work. Even more, Father, give us your help in good times and bad, in our weakness, our failures, and our sins. You know that we cannot bear our burdens alone. We are only little children, and the world seems very dark to us, and our path very hard, if we are alone. But we are *your* little children; and so we know we can come to our Father, to ask you to help us, give us new energy, and strength, and give us hope. We are not ashamed of our tears, for our Lord has wept with us. We do not ask you to take away our sorrow, for Jesus was made perfect through suffering. But we do ask you to be with us as you were with him, dear Father, close to your little ones, just as he promised you would be. Amen.

The Altar at Rome, 1862, adapted

Jesus prayed for those who would live by faith. Do you think the modern world is still a "dark place" and a "hard way" for people who live by faith? Why?

He is the image of the invisible God, the firstborn over all creation. For by him all things were created: things in heaven and on earth, visible and invisible, whether thrones or powers or rulers or authorities; all things were created by him and for him. He is before all things, and in him all things hold together. And he is the head of the body, the church; he is the beginning and the firstborn from among the dead, so that in everything he might have the supremacy. For God was pleased to have all his fullness dwell in him, and through him to reconcile to himself all things, whether things on earth or things in heaven, by making peace through his blood, shed on the cross.

Colossians 1:15-20

Teach us, Holy Father, to hope in your name, from whom
  everything that exists has come.
Open our inward eyes to recognize you, although you are the
  highest in high heaven, and the most holy.
You, Lord God, bring down the proud and outwit the cunning;
  promote the humble, and make the arrogant fall;
  hold in your hand every issue of life—
  whether we are to be rich or poor,
  whether we are to live or die;
  see every spirit, good or evil,
  and the inner thoughts and intentions of every person.
If we are in danger, you come to our aid.
If we are feeling desperate, you save us from our own sense of
  failure.
If events in the world overshadow us, we remember that you are
  the creator and overseer of every living being.

Clement of Rome (1st century A.D.), adapted

*As you think about the world, in what areas are you most grateful to
know that Christ holds all things together?*

For you created my inmost being; you knit me together in my mother's womb.

I praise you because I am fearfully and wonderfully made; your works are wonderful, I know that full well.

My frame was not hidden from you when I was made in the secret place.

When I was woven together in the depths of the earth, your eyes saw my unformed body.

All the days ordained for me were written in your book before one of them came to be.

Psalm 139:13-16

Litany of Dedication

Father: In you, Lord, we all have our beginnings.
Mother: And we thank you for creating new life.
Father: We praise your greatness in granting us this, your gift.
Mother: We ask for your sustaining grace in caring for this child.
Father: Bless this child with your presence.
Mother: Enfold him/her in your mercy.
Father: May he/she be one in whom your glory dwells.
Mother: We pray for parenthood love, joy, and peace.
Father: We pray for parenthood meekness, mercy, and self control.
Mother: We praise you, we thank you, we bow in childlike awe before your greatness.
Together: We dedicate this child to you.

Adapted from *Loving Your Preborn Baby*

What does it mean to you to know that God "knit you together" in your mother's womb?

A Christian who doesn't amount to much in this world should be glad, for he is great in the Lord's sight. But a rich man should be glad that his riches mean nothing to the Lord, for he will soon be gone, like a flower that has lost its beauty and fades away, withered—killed by the scorching summer sun. So it is with rich men. They will soon die and leave behind all their busy activities.

James 1:9-11, TLB

Look in great mercy upon your people gathered here. Some of them are full of joy. You have filled their sky with stars. Their way is bright with inward joy and with surrounding comforts. May they not begin to worship their comforts, nor turn their worship to the stars, nor begin to make a god of the things around them. O Lord, keep your people in the hour of prosperity. May our hearts never wander from the living God, and may we walk as much by faith in the unseen as we should do if we were in the dark.

Charles Spurgeon (1834-1892), adapted

If you were assigned to live in a primitive place, what comforts would you miss most? How can you avoid placing your security in material things?

The LORD is my
rock, my fortress
and my deliverer;
my God is my rock, in whom
I take refuge.

He is my shield and the
horn of my salvation, my
stronghold.

I call to the LORD, who is
worthy of praise, and I am
saved from my enemies.

Psalm 18:2-3

Write your blessed name, O Lord, upon our hearts, there to be engraved so deeply that no prosperity or adversity shall ever move us from your love. Be our strong Tower of defense, a Comforter in tribulation, a Deliverer in distress, a very present Help in trouble, and a Guide to heaven through the many temptations and dangers of this life. Amen.

Thomas à Kempis, (c. 1380-1471), adapted

Do you see God as being involved in your life? Has there been a time when you felt you have been supernaturally protected from danger or evil?

PURITY

He committed no sin, and no deceit was found in his mouth. When they hurled their insults at him, he did not retaliate; when he suffered, he made no threats.... He himself bore our sins in his body on the tree, so that we might die to sins and live for righteousness; by his wounds you have been healed.

1 Peter 2:22-24

Fairest Lord Jesus, Ruler of all nature,
O Thou of God and man the Son:
Thee will I cherish, Thee will I honor.
Thou my soul's glory, joy, and crown.

Fair are the meadows, Fairer still the woodlands,
Robed in the blooming garb of spring;
Jesus is fairer, Jesus is purer,
Who makes the woeful heart to sing.

Fair is the sunshine, Fairer still the moon light,
And all the twinkling starry host;
Jesus shines brighter, Jesus shines purer
Than all the angels heaven can boast.

Beautiful Savior! Lord of the nations!
Son of God and Son of Man!
Glory and honor, Praise, adoration,
Now and forevermore be Thine! Amen.

From *Münster Gesangbuch*

Is it really possible to have a pure life like Jesus' life, as the Bible passage describes? What do you think it requires?

he LORD is my shepherd, I shall not be in want.

He makes me lie down in green pastures, he leads me beside quiet waters, he restores my soul.

He guides me in paths of righteousness for his name's sake.

Even though I walk through the valley of the shadow of death,

I will fear no evil, for you are with me; your rod and your staff, they comfort me.

You prepare a table before me in the presence of my enemies.

You anoint my head with oil; my cup overflows.

Surely goodness and love will follow me all the days of my life, and I will dwell in the house of the LORD forever.

Psalm 23

Dear God, our entire lives have been journeys of mercies and blessings shown to those most undeserving of them. Year after year you have carried us on, removed dangers from our paths, refreshed us, been patient with us, directed us, sustained us. O, don't leave us when we are weak and faithless. We know you will stay with us, that we can rest assured in you. As we are true to your ways, you will, to the very end, be superabundantly good to us. We may rest upon your arm; we can sleep like babies in their mothers' laps. Amen.

John Henry Newman (1801-1890), adapted

If you were to rewrite this psalm to fit your life now, how would it begin?
"The Lord is my _____."

ORD, you have been our dwelling place throughout all generations.

Teach us to number our days aright, that we may gain a heart of wisdom.

May your deeds be shown to your servants, your splendor to their children.

May the favor of the Lord our God rest upon us; establish the work of our hands for us—yes, establish the work of our hands.

Psalm 90:1, 12, 16-17

Lord, in a world that worships youthfulness and overachievement, we thank you for the ability to see life in a different way. We thank you for the seasons that make time so rich and full of discovery. We are grateful that so many of the saints in history and especially in Scripture were clearly beyond retirement age when they made important contributions to your kingdom. Father, we thank you for the testimony of (name)'s life of hard work and that he/she now has the opportunity of a freer schedule and some long-awaited rest and change. Open his/her eyes to see all that you have planned for this phase of life. Fill his/her heart with great expectation and confidence and a willingness to continue to hear your voice and follow where you lead. We ask for bodily and mental strength, and for continued grace and growing contentment, so that (name)'s light may shine in a world full of bitterness and wasted abilities. Amen.

How has the retiree's life been an inspiration or encouragement to you?

ut God loved us with so much love that he was generous with his mercy: when we were dead through our sins, he brought us to life with Christ—it is through grace that you have been saved— and raised us up with him and gave us a place with him in heaven, in Christ Jesus. This was to show for all ages to come, through his goodness toward us in Christ Jesus, how infinitely rich he is in grace. Because it is by grace that you have been saved, through faith; not by anything of your own, but by a gift from God; not by anything that you have done, so that nobody can claim the credit. We are God's work of art, created in Christ Jesus to live the good life as from the beginning he had meant us to live it.

Ephesians 2:4-10, JB

O Lord Jesus, our souls fly to you. You are the only safe place for our hearts. Our confidence is fixed upon your shed blood and righteousness, and we believe that these will never fail us. We are persuaded that if we build upon this Rock of ages, the floods may come, and the winds may beat upon that house, but it shall not fall because it is built upon the rock. Renew the faith of your people. Let its former simplicity come back. May we each of us come to Jesus as we did at first, weary, and overworn, and sad, and sinful, and find in him all that our largest want can possibly demand. Oh for grace today to take a bleeding Savior at his word, and to believe him to be the propitiation for our sins.

Charles Spurgeon (1834-1892), adapted

If you knew you would die today, what would you do?

hen I saw a great white throne and him who was seated on it. Earth and sky fled from his presence, and there was no place for them. And I saw the dead, great and small, standing before the throne, and books were opened. Another book was opened, which is the book of life. The dead were judged according to what they had done as recorded in the books. The sea gave up the dead that were in it, and death and Hades gave up the dead that were in them, and each person was judged according to what he had done.

Revelation 20:11-13

LORD—
You examine us and know us,
   you know if we are standing or sitting,
   you read our thoughts from far away,
   whether we walk or lie down, you are watching,
   you know every detail of our conduct . . .
Examine us and know our hearts,
   probe us and know our thoughts;
   make sure we do not follow harmful ways,
   and guide us in the way that is everlasting.

Psalm 139:1-3, 23-24, adapted

When was the last time your work or your character was evaluated by another person? How did it feel, and what were the results?

Suppose one of you had a servant plowing or looking after the sheep. Would he say to the servant when he comes in from the field, "Come along now and sit down to eat"? Would he not rather say, "Prepare my supper, get yourself ready and wait on me while I eat and drink; after that you may eat and drink"? Would he thank the servant because he did what he was told to do? So you also, when you have done everything you were told to do, should say, "We are unworthy servants; we have only done our duty."

Luke 17:7-10

Teach us, good Lord, to serve you as you deserve; to give and not to count the cost; to fight and not to mind the wounds; to work hard and not to ask for rest; to labor and not to ask for any reward save knowing that we do as you wish. Through Jesus Christ our Lord.

Ignatius of Loyola (1491-1556), adapted

What do you consider your God-given gifts to be? How can you serve others?

o you not know? Have you not heard?

The LORD is the everlasting God, the Creator of the ends of the earth.

He will not grow tired or weary, and his understanding no one can fathom.

He gives strength to the weary and increases the power of the weak.

Even youths grow tired and weary, and young men stumble and fall; but those who hope in the LORD will renew their strength.

They will soar on wings like eagles; they will run and not grow weary, they will walk and not be faint.

Isaiah 40:28-31

O Father of mercies and God of all comfort, our only help in this time of need: we ask that you visit (name) and take away this sickness. Look upon him/her with the eyes of your mercy; comfort him/her with a sense of your love; preserve him/her from the temptations of the enemy; and give him/her patience under this affliction. In your good time, restore him/her to health and enable him/her to lead the rest of his/her life to your glory. Grant that finally (name) may dwell with you in life everlasting, through Jesus Christ our Lord. Amen.

From *Promises & Prayers for Healing*

If someone wanted to help energize you during a weary time, what could that person do for you?

emember your
Creator in the
days of your
youth, before the days of
trouble come and the years
approach when you will say,
"I find no pleasure in them."
Remember him—before the
silver cord is severed, or the
golden bowl is broken;
before the pitcher is shattered at the spring, or the
wheel broken at the well,
and the dust returns to the
ground it came from, and
the spirit returns to God who
gave it.

Ecclesiastes 12:1, 6-7

You are the fountain of life; in you we live, move, and have our being . . . . You send your Spirit and renew the face of the earth; and, from apparent death, all nature starts into reanimated vigor and joy. . . . The whole earth is full of your riches.

While we enjoy the freshness of this season, bless us also with the renewing of the Holy Spirit. May old things pass away, and all become new in Christ; may the beauty of the Lord be upon us; and the joy of the Lord be our strength.

May the young remember that they are now in the spring of life; and that this spring, once gone, can never be regained. Help them to use the time wisely, for the cultivation of their minds, the formation of their habits, the correction of their tempers, their preparation for future usefulness, and their gaining that good part which shall not be taken away from them.

Albert Barnes (1798-1870), adapted

If you could live any part of your life over again, which part would it be? What would you do differently?

I will never forget your precepts, for by them you have preserved my life. . . .

To all perfection I see a limit; but your commands are boundless.

Oh, how I love your law! I meditate on it all day long. Your commands make me wiser than my enemies, for they are ever with me.

I have more insight than all my teachers, for I meditate on your statutes.

I have more understanding than the elders, for I obey your precepts. . . .

I have not departed from your laws, for you yourself have taught me.

How sweet are your words to my taste, sweeter than honey to my mouth!

I gain understanding from your precepts; therefore I hate every wrong path.

Psalm 119:93-104

O God, it is your plan that we work for what we desire in life. Since it is by your blessing that work succeeds, we pray that you will look with mercy on our studies and endeavors. Help us, O Lord, to plan only what is lawful and right; and give us calmness of mind and steadiness of purpose. We pray that we may so do your will in this short life as to obtain happiness in the world to come. For the sake of Jesus Christ our Lord, Amen.

Samuel Johnson (1709-1784), adapted

When you aren't busy, what do you tend to meditate on or mull over in your mind? Are your meditations good for you, or do they need to be changed into thought patterns that are more positive?

There is a time for everything, and a season for every activity under heaven:
a time to be born and a time to die,
a time to plant and a time to uproot,
a time to kill and a time to heal,
a time to tear down and a time to build,
a time to weep and a time to laugh,
a time to mourn and a time to dance,
a time to scatter stones and a time to gather them,
a time to embrace and a time to refrain,
a time to search and a time to give up,
a time to keep and a time to throw away,
a time to tear and a time to mend,
a time to be silent and a time to speak,
a time to love and a time to hate,
a time for war and a time for peace.

Ecclesiastes 3:1-8

O Lord, let us not desire health or life, except to spend them for you, with you, and in you. You alone know what is good for us; so do what seems best to you. Give to us, or take from us; conform our wills to yours; and enable us to receive with true humility the orders that will accomplish your divine plan. And may we accept all that comes from you, through Jesus Christ our Lord. Amen.

Blaise Pascal (1623-1662), adapted

What word or phrase best describes the emotional or spiritual season you are in presently?

s long as the earth endures, seedtime and harvest, cold and heat, summer and winter, day and night will never cease.

Genesis 8:22

You have been a refuge for the poor, a refuge for the needy in his distress, a shelter from the storm and a shade from the heat.

Isaiah 25:4

We praise you for the seasons of the year. How wise, and useful, and necessary, are these intermingled rains and sunbeams— may Jesus, as the Sun of Righteousness, arise upon us, with healing under his wings; and may he come down as rain upon the mown grass, and as showers that water the earth.

When we walk by the cool stream—may we think of Jesus, who gives us living water so that we never thirst again.

When we retire from the scorching heat of the day, into the inviting shade—may we be thankful for a rest at noon, a shelter from the heat, and that you, Lord, are our refuge always.

Albert Barnes (1798-1870), adapted

How does knowing that God planned the seasons affect your attitude toward them?

But there is one thing, my friends, that you must never forget: that with the Lord, "a day" can mean a thousand years, and a thousand years is like a day. The Lord is not being slow to carry out his promises, as anybody else might be called slow; but he is being patient with you all, wanting nobody to be lost and everybody to be brought to change his ways. The Day of the Lord will come like a thief, and then with a roar the sky will vanish, the elements will catch fire and fall apart, the earth and all that it contains will be burned up. Since everything is coming to an end like this, you should be living holy and saintly lives while you wait and long for the Day of God to come . . . So then, my friends, while you are waiting, do your best to live lives without spot or stain so that he will find you at peace.

2 Peter 3:8-14, JB

Great God of wonders, your nature is infinite, and everything
that flows out of it is infinite also.
With you everything that will happen has already happened.
You appear at the beginning and at the end of time
simultaneously; the Alpha and Omega are one and the same.
With you, endlessness flows into time, even as time shall again
flow into endlessness.
You have already lived all our tomorrows in the same way you
have lived all our yesterdays.
We praise you for this, which is so far beyond our capacity to
comprehend.

Isaiah 46:9-10, paraphrased by Robert C. Savage (1914-1987)

*Why have science fiction stories and movies about time travel remained
so popular? What difference would it make if there were no distinctions
between past, present, and future?*

ou then, my son, be strong in the grace that is in Christ Jesus. . . . Endure hardship with us like a good soldier of Christ Jesus. No one serving as a soldier gets involved in civilian affairs—he wants to please his commanding officer. Similarly, if anyone competes as an athlete, he does not receive the victor's crown unless he competes according to the rules. The hardworking farmer should be the first to receive a share of the crops.

2 Timothy 2:1, 3-7

O Father, this week may bring some hard task to our lives, or some hard trial to our love. We may grow weary, or sad, or hopeless in our situation. But, Father, our whole life until now has been one great proof of your care. Food has come for our bodies, thoughts to our minds, love to our hearts—and all of it is from you. So please help us, while we stand still on this side of all that the day may bring, to resolve that we will trust you this day to shine into any gloom of the mind, to stand by us in any trial of our love, and to give us rest in your good time as we need. May this day be full of a power that shall bring us near to you, and make us more like you. Amen.

Robert Collyer, adapted

In your own experiences, what has made your faith or trust grow stronger?

At this point many of his disciples turned away and deserted him. Then Jesus turned to the Twelve and asked, "Are you going too?" Simon Peter replied, "Master, to whom shall we go? You alone have the words that give eternal life, and we believe them and know you are the holy Son of God."

John 6:66-68, TLB

O Lord Jesus Christ, you have said that you are the way, the truth, and the life. Do not allow us to wander from you, who are the way, nor to distrust you, who are the truth, nor to rest in anything other than you, who are the life.

Desiderius Erasmus (c. 1466-1536), adapted

Most of us believe and live out what our culture and family have taught us to believe and live. Has there ever been a time when you came to an acute point of decision about Jesus, as these disciples did?

To you whom I love I say, let us go on loving one another, for love comes from God. Every man who truly loves is God's son and knows him. But the man who does not love cannot know him at all, for God is love. To us, the greatest demonstration of God's love for us has been his sending his only Son into the world to give us life through him. We see real love, not in the fact that we loved God, but that he loved us and sent his Son to make personal atonement for our sins. If God loved us as much as that, surely we, in our turn, should love each other!

1 John 4:7-11, PHILLIPS

Dear Father, from whom the marriage union derives its beauty and its divine purpose, we thank you for the love that has grown between these two people and for the commitment they have made to one another. Bless their commitment and fill their union with grace and joy. Grow them together into the image of your own nature. Give them the grace to forgive and receive forgiveness, a love that overflows to others around them, and a home that is a haven of blessing and peace. Make this relationship a living and a constant proof of your power to transform lives and of the possibilities that come with love that humbly submits and seeks the other's good. We thank you for this mystery of unity and joy that shows us something about your love and commitment to us, your people. Amen.

What words of advice would you offer to newlyweds?

L ove is patient, love is kind. It does not envy, it does not boast, it is not proud. It is not rude, it is not self-seeking, it is not easily angered, it keeps no record of wrongs. Love does not delight in evil but rejoices with the truth. It always protects, always trusts, always hopes, always perseveres.

1 Corinthians 13:4-7

Dear God, who created the marriage union, we are grateful for the joy and fulfillment this relationship provides. We thank you for the milestones that have been crossed during the past year, of the love that has grown, the loyalty that has been strengthened, and the dreams that have been given birth. We pray that you will bless this couple's union with increasing wisdom, love, and grace. We ask that their growth together will be a picture of your love and commitment to us, your people. Give them strength for the trials that are inevitable during this life; fill their hearts with joy. Grant them wisdom to cheer and encourage one another and for each to help the other toward goals in career, faith, and character.

What do you think are some key ingredients to a good and lasting marriage?

The day is Yours, the
night also is Yours;
You have prepared
the light and the sun.
You have set all the borders
of the earth;
You have made summer and
winter.

Psalm 74:16-17, NKJV

O God of nature and providence; many are your works; in wisdom you have made them all, and all are full of your goodness. The welfare of your creation requires the severity of winter as well as the pleasures of spring. We praise you in every season.

We thank you for a house to shelter us, for clothes to cover us, for fuel to warm us, and all those things that allow us to live even in the coldest and darkest of times.

May we be grateful. May we reflect on the condition of those who do not have shelter or food—and waste nothing; hoard nothing; but do our best to be ministers of mercy, in the name of Jesus.

Albert Barnes (1798-1870), adapted

What temptations and tests of your faith come to you especially during winter? What problems are peculiar to spring? The other seasons?

ll these people were still living by faith when they died. They did not receive the things promised; they only saw them and welcomed them from a distance. And they admitted that they were aliens and strangers on earth. . . . If they had been thinking of the country they had left, they would have had opportunity to return. Instead, they were longing for a better country—a heavenly one. Therefore God is not ashamed to be called their God, for he has prepared a city for them.

Hebrews 11:13-16

Dear Lord, show me myself. Tell me where I grieve you. I feel within me the pull of the world and I am both ashamed and weak. I *want* to obey you and yet I find myself craving the things the world offers as well.

Lord, make heaven *real* to me. Teach me to know at the very center of my being that my true citizenship is in heaven, not here on earth. Thank you for the material blessings you have poured on me, but tear the attraction for them from my heart so that I become truly indifferent to wealth, or poverty, and am free to abound or to be in want, indifferent to every circumstance in life except only that I may hold your hand and walk beside you. Show me that the world is a fickle and false companion, and a cruel master. Keep me loyal to you.

John White

Think of the most contented person you know. How does he or she maintain such an attitude?

HOLIDAYS

in order of the calendar year

ecause of the LORD'S great love we are not consumed, for his compassions never fail. They are new every morning; great is your faithfulness. I say to myself, "The LORD is my portion; therefore I will wait for him."

Lamentations 3:22-24

Most gracious God, you have been infinitely merciful to us, not only in the past year, but through all the years of our life. Be pleased to accept our genuine thanks for your innumerable blessings to us. Graciously pardon our past sins and generously give us all those graces and virtues that will make us acceptable to you. And for every year you are pleased to add to our lives, add also, we humbly pray, more strength to our faith, more intensity to our love, and a greater perfection to our obedience. Help us to serve you most faithfully the remainder of our lives, for Jesus Christ's sake. Amen.

Charles Now, adapted

What signs of God's faithfulness have you seen during the past year?

A new command-
ment I give to you,
that you love one
another; as I have loved you,
that you also love one another. By this all will know
that you are My disciples, if
you have love for one an-
other.

John 13:34-35, NKJV

Oh God, the Father of all, you ask every one of us to spread
Love where the poor are humiliated,
Joy where the Church is brought low,
And reconciliation where people are divided . . . father against
son, mother against daughter, husband against wife,
believers against those who cannot believe, Christians against
their unloved fellow Christians.
You open this way for us, so that the wounded body of Jesus
Christ, your Church, may be leaven for the poor of the earth
and in the whole human family.

Mother Teresa and Brother Roger of Taizé

What are some practical ways you can demonstrate the love of God?

y prayer is not for them alone. I pray also for those who will believe in me through their message, that all of them may be one, Father, just as you are in me and I am in you. May they also be in us so that the world may believe that you have sent me. I have given them the glory that you gave me, that they may be one as we are one: I in them and you in me. May they be brought to complete unity to let the world know that you sent me and have loved them even as you have loved me.

John 17:20-23

Loving Father,
You have made all humanity in your likeness and love all you have made; do not let the world separate itself from you by building barriers of race and color.

As your Son, Our Savior, was born of a Hebrew mother, yet rejoiced in the faith of a Syrian woman and a Roman soldier, welcomed the Greeks who sought him, and had his cross carried by an African, so teach us rightly to recognize the members of all races as fellow-heirs to your kingdom. We ask this in the name of Christ Jesus, the Prince of Peace. Amen.

The Religious Society of Friends in South Africa

According to these verses, why do you think it so important for Christians to be unified in Jesus?

My dear children, I write this to you so that you will not sin. But if anybody does sin, we have one who speaks to the Father in our defense—Jesus Christ, the Righteous One. He is the atoning sacrifice for our sins, and not only for ours but also for the sins of the whole world. We know that we have come to know him if we obey his commands. The man who says, "I know him," but does not do what he commands is a liar, and the truth is not in him. But if anyone obeys his word, God's love is truly made complete in him. This is how we know we are in him: Whoever claims to live in him must walk as Jesus did.

1 John 2:1-6

Thanks be to you, our Lord Jesus Christ,
   for all the benefits which you have given us,
   for all the pains and insults which you have borne for us.
Most merciful Redeemer, Friend, and Brother,
   may we know you more clearly,
   love you more dearly,
   and follow you more nearly, day by day.

   St. Richard (1197-1253)

   What do you think "sin" is? How do you deal with your own sin?

Surely he took up our infirmities and carried our sorrows, yet we considered him stricken by God, smitten by him, and afflicted. But he was pierced for our transgressions, he was crushed for our iniquities; the punishment that brought us peace was upon him, and by his wounds we are healed. We all, like sheep, have gone astray, each of us has turned to his own way; and the LORD has laid on him the iniquity of us all.

Isaiah 53:4-6

ome, Lord Jesus!

ome, Lord Jesus! Do I dare
ry: Lord Jesus, quickly come!
ash the lightning in the air,
rash the thunder on my home!
nould I speak this aweful prayer?
ome, Lord Jesus, help me dare.

ome, Lord Jesus! Come this night
ith your purging and your power,
or the earth is dark with blight
nd in sin we run and cower
efore the splendid, raging sight
f the breaking of the night.

Come, my Lord! Our darkness end!
Break the bonds of time and space.
All the powers of evil rend
By the radiance of your face.
The laughing stars with joy attend:
Come Lord Jesus! Be my end!

Madeleine L'Engle

From this Bible passage, how would you explain to someone else the meaning of Jesus' death?

We love because he first loved us. If anyone says, "I love God," yet hates his brother, he is a liar. For anyone who does not love his brother, whom he has seen, cannot love God, whom he has not seen. And he has given us this command: Whoever loves God must also love his brother.

1 John 4:19-21

O God, we have known and believed the love that you have for us. Help us to live in you, and you in us. May we learn to love you whom we have not seen, by loving our brethren whom we have seen. Teach us, O heavenly Father, the love wherewith you have loved us; fashion us, O blessed Lord, after your own example of love; shed abroad, O Holy Spirit of Love, the love of God and man in our hearts. Amen.

Henry Alford (1810-1871), adapted

What is the test of love stated in these verses? According to this test, how are you doing at loving God?

Do everything without complaining or arguing, so that you may become blameless and pure, children of God without fault in a crooked and depraved generation, in which you shine like stars in the universe as you hold out the word of life—in order that I may boast on the day of Christ that I did not run or labor for nothing.

Philippians 2:14-16

Lord, make me an instrument of thy peace.
Where there is hatred, let me sow love;
Where there is injury, pardon;
Where there is doubt, faith;
Where there is despair, hope;
Where there is darkness, light;
Where there is sadness, joy.

O Divine master, grant that I may not so much seek
To be consoled, as to console;
Not so much to be understood as to understand;
Not so much to be loved as to love;
For it is in giving that we receive;
It is in pardoning that we are pardoned;
It is in dying that we awaken to eternal life.

St. Francis of Assisi (1182-1226)

How can you be an instrument of peace in someone's life this week?

or this reason I kneel before the Father, from whom his whole family in heaven and on earth derives its name. I pray that out of his glorious riches he may strengthen you with power through his Spirit in your inner being, so that Christ may dwell in your hearts through faith. And I pray that you, being rooted and established in love, may have power, together with all the saints, to grasp how wide and long and high and deep is the love of Christ, and to know this love that surpasses knowledge—that you may be filled to the measure of all the fullness of God. Now to him who is able to do immeasurably more than all we ask or imagine, according to his power that is at work within us, to him be glory in the church and in Christ Jesus throughout all generations, for ever and ever! Amen.

Ephesians 3:14-20

Christ Be with Me

I arise today through God's strength to pilot me,
God's might to uphold me,
God's wisdom to guide me,
God's eye to look before me,
God's ear to hear me,
God's word to speak for me,
God's hand to guard me,
God's way to lie before me,
God's shield to protect me.
Christ be with me, Christ before me, Christ behind me,
Christ in me, Christ beneath me, Christ above me,
Christ on my right, Christ on my left,
Christ when I lie down, Christ when I sit down, Christ when I arise,
Christ in the heart of every one who thinks of me,
Christ in the mouth of every one who speaks of me,
Christ in every eye that sees me,
Christ in every ear that hears me

St. Patrick (c. 390–c. 461)

In what tasks or areas of your life do you especially need God's power this week?

The disciples went and did as Jesus had instructed them. They brought the donkey and the colt, placed their cloaks on them, and Jesus sat on them. A very large crowd spread their cloaks on the road, while others cut branches from the trees and spread them on the road. The crowds that went ahead of him and those that followed shouted, "Hosanna to the Son of David!" "Blessed is he who comes in the name of the Lord!" "Hosanna in the highest!" When Jesus entered Jerusalem, the whole city was stirred and asked, "Who is this?" The crowds answered, "This is Jesus, the prophet from Nazareth in Galilee."

Matthew 21:6-11

Ride on! ride on in majesty!
In lowly pomp ride on to die;
O Christ, Thy triumphs now begin
O'er captive death and conquered sin.

Ride on! ride on in majesty!
The angel armies of the sky
Look down with sad and wondering eyes
To see the approaching sacrifice.

Ride on! ride on in majesty!
The last and fiercest strife is nigh;
The Father on His sapphire throne
Awaits His own anointed Son.

Ride on! ride on in majesty!
In lowly pomp ride on to die;
Bow Thy meek head to mortal pain,
Then take, O God, Thy power, and reign.

Henry Hart Milman (1791-1868)

Most people in the Western world do not know how to relate to kingship today. What kind of king does Jesus seem to be?

You see, at just the right time, when we were still powerless, Christ died for the ungodly. . . . God demonstrates his own love for us in this: While we were still sinners, Christ died for us. Since we have now been justified by his blood, how much more shall we be saved from God's wrath through him! For if, when we were God's enemies, we were reconciled to him through the death of his Son, how much more, having been reconciled, shall we be saved through his life! Not only is this so, but we also rejoice in God through our Lord Jesus Christ, through whom we have now received reconciliation.

Romans 5:6-11

Today he who hung the earth upon the waters is hung upon
the Cross.
He who is King of the angels is arrayed in a crown of thorns.
He who wraps the heaven in clouds is wrapped in the purple of
mockery.
He who in Jordan set Adam free receives blows upon his face.
The Bridegroom of the Church is transfixed with nails.
The Son of the Virgin is pierced with a spear.
We worship you, Lord Jesus.
Draw us to yourself with bands of love.
Show us the glory of your Resurrection.

A hymn of Good Friday, Orthodox Tradition

What does Christ's death mean to you?

nd if Christ has not been raised, our preaching is useless and so is your faith. More than that, we are then found to be false witnesses about God, for we have testified about God that he raised Christ from the dead. . . . And if Christ has not been raised your faith is futile; you are still in your sins. Then those also who have fallen asleep in Christ are lost. If only for this life we have hope in Christ, we are to be pitied more than all men. But Christ has indeed been raised from the dead, the firstfruits of those who have fallen asleep.

1 Corinthians 15:14-20

Thine be the glory, risen, conquering Son,
Endless is the victory Thou o'er death hast won;
Angels in bright raiment rolled the stone away,
Kept the folded grave-clothes, where Thy body lay.

Lo! Jesus meets us risen from the tomb;
Lovingly he greets us, scatters fear and gloom;
Let the church with gladness, hymns of triumph sing,
For the Lord now liveth, death hath lost its sting.

No more we doubt Thee, glorious Prince of life;
Life is nought without Thee; aid us in our strife,
Make us more than conquerors, through Thy deathless love;
Bring us safe through Jordan to Thy home above.

Edmond Louis Budry, translated by Richard Birch Hoyle

Think of two words that describe Easter especially well for you.

All this I have spoken while still with you. But the Counselor, the Holy Spirit, whom the Father will send in my name, will teach you all things and will remind you of everything I have said to you. Peace I leave with you; my peace I give you. I do not give to you as the world gives. Do not let your hearts be troubled and do not be afraid.

John 14:25-27

O Lord, grant that our hearts may be truly cleansed and filled with your Holy Spirit, so that we may serve you. Help us to lie down to sleep in entire confidence in you and submission to your will, ready for life or for death. Let us live for the day we're given, not overcharged with worldly cares. Remind us that our treasure is not here, and give us the desire to join you in your heavenly kingdom along with those who are already with you. O Lord, save us from sin, and guide us with your Spirit. Keep us in faithful obedience to you, through Jesus Christ your Son, our Lord. Amen.

Thomas Arnold (1795-1842)

What do you think is the difference between "worldly" peace and having the peace of God? Between worldly power and God's power?

s a prisoner for the Lord, then, I urge you to live a life worthy of the calling you have received. Be completely humble and gentle; be patient, bearing with one another in love. Make every effort to keep the unity of the Spirit through the bond of peace. There is one body and one Spirit—just as you were called to one hope when you were called—one Lord, one faith, one baptism; one God and Father of all, who is over all and through all and in all.

Ephesians 4:1-6

You are Three and One, Lord God, all good.
You are good, all good, supreme good, Lord God, living
and true.
You are love, you are wisdom.
You are humility, you are endurance.
You are rest, you are peace.
You are joy and gladness.
You are justice and moderation.
You are all our riches, and you suffice for us.
You are beauty, you are gentleness.
You are our protector, you are our guardian and defender.
You are courage, you are our haven and our hope.
You are our faith, our great consolation.
You are our eternal life, great and wonderful Lord,
God Almighty, Merciful Savior.

St. Francis of Assisi (1182-1226)

*Do you pray to all three persons of the Trinity? Which of the three do you
relate to most often in your prayers?*

ho shall separate us from the love of Christ? Shall trouble or hardship or persecution or famine or nakedness or danger or sword? . . . No, in all these things we are more than conquerors through him who loved us. For I am convinced that neither death nor life, neither angels nor demons, neither the present nor the future, nor any powers, neither height nor depth, nor anything else in all creation, will be able to separate us from the love of God that is in Christ Jesus our Lord.

Romans 8:35-39

Lord, behold our family here assembled.
We thank you for this place in which we dwell,
   for the love that unites us,
   for the peace accorded us this day,
   for the hope with which we expect the morrow;
   for the health, the work, the food and the bright skies that
   make our lives delightful . . .
Bless us, if it may be, in all our innocent endeavors; if it may
not, give us the strength to endure that which is to come, that
we may be
   brave in peril,
   constant in tribulation,
   temperate in wrath,
and in all changes of fortune and down to the gates of death,
   loyal and loving to one another.

Robert Louis Stevenson (1850-1894)

Imagine the worst situation your family could face. How can these verses in Romans encourage you?

I eagerly expect and hope that I will in no way be ashamed, but will have sufficient courage so that now as always Christ will be exalted in my body, whether by life or by death. For to me, to live is Christ and to die is gain.

Philippians 1:20-21

We do not ask, O Father, for health or life. We make an offering to you of all our days. You have counted them. We would know nothing more. All we ask is to die rather than live unfaithful to you; and, if it be your will that we depart, let us die in patience and love. Almighty God, you hold in your hand the keys of the grave to open and close it at your will. Do not give us life if we shall love it too well. Living or dying we would be yours. Amen.

Francois de la Mothe Fenelon (1651-1715), adapted

What is it that you are living for? What would you be willing to give your life for?

hildren, obey your parents in the Lord, for this is right. "Honor your father and mother"—which is the first commandment with a promise—"that it may go well with you and that you may enjoy long life on the earth." Fathers, do not exasperate your children; instead, bring them up in the training and instruction of the Lord.

Ephesians 6:1-4

We pray that you will give all children grace to reverently love their parents and lovingly to obey them. Teach us all that family duty never ends or lessens: and bless all parents in their children, and all children in their parents. Thank you that the fatherless find mercy in you. Help them to be loving and dutiful to you, their true Father. May your will be their law, your house their home, your love their inheritance. And I earnestly pray that you will comfort those who have lost their children. Grant us all faith to yield our dearest treasures to you with joy and thanksgiving, that where our treasure is, there our hearts may be also. Amen.

Christina G. Rossetti (1830-1894), adapted

What are some differences between Hollywood-TV families and your real-life family? How can the guidelines in Ephesians 6 help your family relationships?

Submit yourselves for the Lord's sake to every authority instituted among men: whether to the king, as the supreme authority, or to governors, who are sent by him to punish those who do wrong and to commend those who do right. For it is God's will that by doing good you should silence the ignorant talk of foolish men. Live as free men, but do not use your freedom as a cover-up for evil; live as servants of God. Show proper respect to everyone: Love the brotherhood of believers, fear God, honor the king.

1 Peter 2:13-17

Almighty God, you are the Giver of all Wisdom. Enlighten my understanding with knowledge of right, and govern my will by your laws. I pray that no deceit may mislead me, nor temptation corrupt me, that I may always endeavor to do good, and to hinder evil. Amidst all the hopes and fears of this world, do not take your Holy Spirit from me, but grant that my thoughts may be fixed on you, the source of everlasting happiness. For Jesus Christ's sake, Amen.

Samuel Johnson (1709-1784), adapted

What do you think it means to live as free people, yet as servants of God?

Let the peace of Christ rule in your hearts, since as members of one body you were called to peace. And be thankful. Let the word of Christ dwell in you richly as you teach and admonish one another with all wisdom, and as you sing psalms, hymns and spiritual songs with gratitude in your hearts to God. And whatever you do, whether in word or deed, do it all in the name of the Lord Jesus, giving thanks to God the Father through him.

Colossians 3:15-17

O Lord, renew our spirits and draw our hearts unto you that our work may not be to us a burden, but a delight; and give us such a mighty love for you as may sweeten all our obedience. Oh, let us not serve you with the spirit of bondage as slaves, but with the cheerfulness and gladness of children, delighting ourselves in you and rejoicing in your work. Amen.

Benjamin Jenks, adapted

How can thankfulness help you do and enjoy your work?

Make a joyful shout to the LORD, all you lands!
Serve the LORD with gladness;
Come before His presence with singing.
Know that the LORD, He is God;
It is He who has made us, and not we ourselves;
We are His people and the sheep of His pasture.

Enter into His gates with thanksgiving,
And into His courts with praise.
Be thankful to Him, and bless His name.
For the LORD is good;
His mercy is everlasting
And His truth endures to all generations.

Psalm 100, NKJV

O Lord our God, let us hope under the shadow of your wings. You will support us, both when we are little, and even when our hair is gray. When our strength comes from you, it is strength; but, when our own, it is feebleness. We return to you, O Lord, that our souls may rise from their weariness toward you. We lean on the things that you have created, and even more on you, who have wonderfully made them; for with you is refreshment and true strength. Amen.

St. Augustine (345-430), adapted

In what ways have you seen God's faithfulness enduring through the generations of your family?

T herefore, since we are surrounded by such a great cloud of witnesses, let us throw off everything that hinders and the sin that so easily entangles, and let us run with perseverance the race marked out for us. Let us fix our eyes on Jesus, the author and perfecter of our faith, who for the joy set before him endured the cross, scorning its shame, and sat down at the right hand of the throne of God.

Hebrews 12:1-2

O thou who wast, and art, and art to come, I thank thee that this Christian way whereon I walk is no untried or uncharted road, but a road beaten hard by the footsteps of saints, apostles, prophets, and martyrs. I thank thee for the finger-posts and danger-signals with which it is marked at every turning and which may be known to me through the study of the Bible, and of all history, and of all the great literature of the world. Beyond all I give thee devout and humble thanks for the great gift of Jesus Christ, the Pioneer of our faith, . . . and that I am not called upon to face any temptation or trial which he did not first endure. Forbid it, Holy Lord, that I should fail to profit by these great memories of the ages that are gone by, . . . through Jesus Christ my Lord. Amen.

John Baillie (1886-1960)

Think of one of your favorite heroes or "saints," from the Bible, history books, or your own circle of friends. Why is this person a favorite?

Everyone must submit himself to the governing authorities, for there is no authority except that which God has established. The authorities that exist have been established by God.

Consequently, he who rebels against the authority is rebelling against what God has instituted, and those who do so will bring judgment on themselves.

Romans 13:1-2

Grant us, Lord, to know all that we should know, to love what we should love, to esteem what most pleases you, and to reject all that is evil in your sight. Let us not judge superficially by what we see, nor be influenced by what we hear from ignorant men, but with true judgment to discern between things spiritual and material, and to seek your will and good pleasure at all times and above all else.

Thomas à Kempis (c. 1380-1471), adapted

Can you think of times when it would be wrong to obey someone in authority over you?

The LORD is the
strength of his
people, a fortress
of salvation for his anointed
one.

Save your people and bless
your inheritance; be their
shepherd and carry them
forever.

Psalm 28:8-9

In these our days so perilous, Lord,
Peace in mercy send us;
No God but thee can fight for us,
No God but thee defend us;
Thou our only God and Savior.

Martin Luther (1483-1546), adapted

*Which image of God means most to you in your present circumstances—
God as your fortress or God as your shepherd? Why?*

Praise the LORD, O my soul; all my inmost being, praise his holy name.

Praise the LORD, O my soul, and forget not all his benefits—

who forgives all your sins and heals all your diseases,

who redeems your life from the pit and crowns you with love and compassion,

who satisfies your desires with good things so that your youth is renewed like the eagle's.

Psalm 103:1-5

What shall I give to him for all his blessing? I can only give my own self—all I have, and all I am. I desire to surrender myself wholly to you, O my God, to live more simply as one set apart for you, not finding my joy and comfort in the earthly blessings you so richly give me, but, while thankful for the gracious gifts, looking only to the Giver as the Source of my happiness and the Object of my life. I cannot shake off the habits of thought and feeling which many years have formed in me; I can only ask you to have mercy on me, poor and needy as I am, and control in me all that is obstinate and sinful. Fill me with your pure and heavenly love, so that all my narrowness and selfishness may be lost in the wideness of your love. Amen.

Maria Hare, adapted

How can you focus more on God himself as the source of your happiness instead of on the material blessings he gives?

But you, Bethlehem Ephrathah, though you are small among the clans of Judah, out of you will come for me one who will be ruler over Israel, whose origins are from of old, from ancient times. Therefore Israel will be abandoned until the time when she who is in labor gives birth and the rest of his brothers return to join the Israelites. He will stand and shepherd his flock in the strength of the LORD, in the majesty of the name of the LORD his God. And they will live securely, for then his greatness will reach to the ends of the earth. And he will be their peace.

Micah 5:2-5

O Morning Star, Splendor of the Light, eternal and bright Sun of Justice; come and enlighten all who live in darkness, and in the shadow of death.
Lord Jesus, come soon!

O King of the nations; you alone can fulfill their desires; Cornerstone, you make opposing nations one; come and save us. You formed us all from the clay.
Lord Jesus, come soon!

O Emmanuel, Hope of the nations and their Savior; come and save us, Lord our God.
Lord Jesus, come soon!

The community of Taizé

Which world events taking place right now remind you of how much the world needs a Savior?

nd there were shepherds living out in the field nearby, keeping watch over their flocks at night. An angel of the Lord appeared to them, and the glory of the Lord shone around them, and they were terrified. But the angel said to them, "Do not be afraid. I bring you good news of great joy that will be for all the people. Today in the town of David a Savior has been born to you; he is Christ the Lord. This will be a sign to you: You will find a baby wrapped in cloths and lying in a manger." Suddenly a great company of the heavenly host appeared with the angel, praising God and saying, "Glory to God in the highest, and on earth peace to men on whom his favor rests."

Luke 2:8-14

We yearn, our Father, for the simple beauty of Christmas—for all the old familiar melodies and words that remind us of that great miracle when he who had made all things was one night to come as a babe, to lie in the crook of a woman's arm.

Before such mystery we kneel, as we follow the shepherds and Wise Men to bring you the gift of our love—a love we confess that has not always been as warm or sincere or real as it should have been. But now, on this Christmas Day, that love would find its Beloved, and from you receive the grace to make it pure again, warm and real.

We bring you our gratitude for every token of your love. Amen.

Peter Marshall (1902-1949)

What does Christmas mean to you? How can you make the Christmas season more meaningful this year?

TABLE GRACES

lmighty God, every creature waits for your care, and you give us our food when it is time. Bless these provisions that are now before us from the harvest of your earth. Let them nourish and strengthen us, so that we can serve you with more energy. Through Jesus Christ.

ather of all light and truth, from whom comes every good and perfect gift, help us to receive with genuine gratefulness and humility the food you have given us. By your grace may we bring honor to your name in whatever we do—as we eat and drink and go about our lives' affairs.

Lord of the harvest, we acknowledge that we depend on you for everything, and the good things in our lives—this food, our home—are gifts and not rewards for our own goodness. Forgive us of the sins we have committed against you today, bless us as we take this food, and through it strengthen us to live in a way that glorifies you. In Jesus' name.

We give you thanks, dear heavenly Father, for the infinite number of gifts you have provided. We especially thank you for the rich provision you made for our souls—salvation through Jesus Christ. Accept our thanks for this food we receive, and help us to prove the sincerity of our gratefulness by holy and obedient lives. Help us to live in this way for Jesus' sake.

ow can we possibly repay you, God, for all that you have done for us? Every day of our lives we are receiving fresh proof of your love. Let your goodness lead us never to pride in our own achievements, but always to repentance for our failures. And if we can do no more than to say "Thank you," help us to do that in sincerity.

e thank you, heavenly Father, for the abundant provision you have made for us; both in our earthly lives and beyond. Thank you for the food we now receive. May your goodness and mercy lead us to want more of your presence and continue to train us for our heavenly destiny, building character that is worthy of your name.

ord, bless the fellowship of this table. We ask that the conversation be as healthy for our spirits as the food is healthy for our bodies. May our words be truthful, uplifting, and our appetites always tempered by faithfulness to your purposes.

ord, we bless your name for this food we now take. Continue to provide for our daily, mundane needs, but more than that, feed us with the Bread of Life. Supply the needs of those who are poor and oppressed in the world, and cause us, as we live well-fed lives, to live in a way that is holy and shows the world your face.

or your great generosity in giving us food this day, we thank you, most merciful Father. And we ask that you feed our minds and spirits also with food that doesn't spoil but lasts forever, so that we may always do what pleases you, through Jesus Christ our Lord.

 ear heavenly Father and merciful God, who opens your hand and replenishes all living creatures with your blessing, we acknowledge our food and drink to be gifts from you, as a father provides for his children's needs. We ask that you bless this meal and give us grace to use it wisely and to be continually thankful. Remind us especially to be generous with neighbors who are poor, through Jesus Christ our Lord.